France

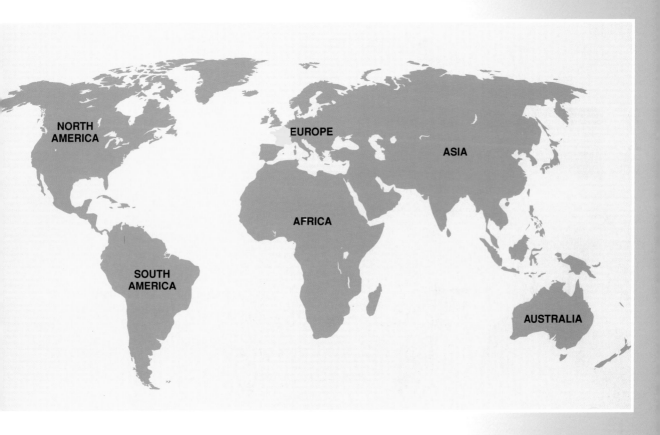

NORTH AMERICA

EUROPE

ASIA

AFRICA

SOUTH AMERICA

AUSTRALIA

Clare Boast

Heinemann Interactive Library
Des Plaines, Illinois

© 1998 Reed Educational & Professional Publishing

Published by Heinemann Interactive Library,
an imprint of Reed Educational & Professional Publishing,
1350 East Touhy Avenue, Suit 240 West, Des Plaines, IL 60018

Produced by Times Offset (M) Sdn. Bhd.
Designed by AMR
Illustrations by Art Construction

02 01 00 99 98
10 9 8 7 6 5 4 3 2 1

Boast, Clare, 1965–
    France / Clare Boast
        p.   cm. – – (Next stop!)
    Includes bibliographical references and index.
    Summary: An introduction to the history, geography, economy, and modern daily life in France.
    ISBN 1-57572-565-7
    1. France – – Juvenile literature.   [1.France.]   I. Title.
II. Series.   97-16748
DC33. 7. B575 1997   C I P
944 – – DC21   AC

Acknowledgments

The author and publisher are grateful to the following for permission to reproduce copyright photographs: ALLSPORT P. Rondeau p.26; Bridgeman Art Library/Giraudon p.29; Colorific! D. Berretty p.18, Boccon-Gibod/Black Star p.23, Carl Purcell p.7; J. Allen Cash Ltd pp.8, 24; Trevor Clifford pp 4, 12–13, 16–17, 19, 21, 25, 26; Robert Harding Picture Library Vandermarst p.14; Trip A. M. Bazalik p.6, C. Bland p.22, D. Brooker p.5, B. Hills p.9, W. Newlands p.20, D. Ray p.28, D. Saunders p.27, A. Tovy pp.10–11; ZEFA p.15.

Cover photograph reproduced with permission of:
   background: Tony Stone Worldwide, Michael Brusselle
   child: Image Bank, Marc Grimberg.

Special thanks to Betty Root for her comments in the preparation of this book.

Every effort has been made to contact copyright holders of any material reproduced in this book. Any omissions will be rectified in subsequent printings if notice is given to the publisher.

Words in the book in bold, **like this**, are explained in the glossary on page 31.

CONTENTS

INTRODUCTION

WHERE IS FRANCE?

France is in the west of Europe. France has borders with six other European countries.

France has coastlines on the Atlantic Ocean, the Mediterranean Sea, and the English Channel. France is joined to England by a tunnel under the English Channel.

The capital city of France is Paris. More than nine million people live there. The Seine River flows through the middle of the city.

The Eiffel Tower, built in 1889, is nearly 1,000 feet high. This is higher than many modern skyscrapers.

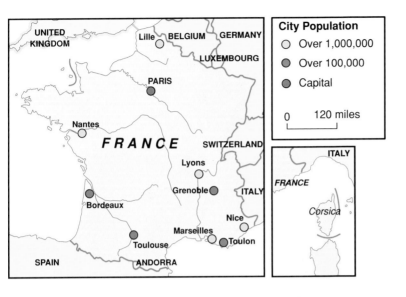

FRANCE'S HISTORY

France was part of the **Roman Empire** for about 500 years. Then it became many different countries. Part of it was ruled by England. France then became one country, ruled by one king. In 1789 there was a **revolution**. Kings were replaced by a **government** chosen by the people.

There are lots of places around the world where the local language is French. This is because France once owned land in Africa, North America and other parts of the world.

The owners of this French castle make their living by selling wine from the grapes they grow.

5

THE LAND

The Ardeche River has worn away the rock to make this gorge in the Massif Central.

PLATEAU

The Massif Central, in the middle and the south of France, is a **plateau**. The plateau is not all flat. There are old **volcanoes**, with lakes in the middle. There are puys. These are steep hills of **lava** from old volcanoes, worn by the weather.

Rivers have also worn away deep **gorges**, like the one in the picture on the left.

MOUNTAINS

France is separated from Spain by the Pyrenees Mountains in the south. The Alps, in the south-east, separate France from Italy and Switzerland.

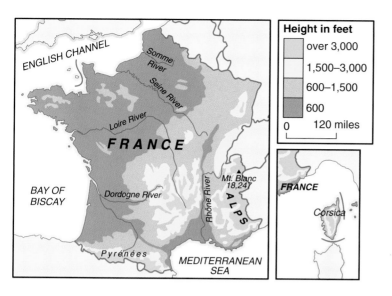

LOWLAND FRANCE

Most people in France live in the low, fairly flat land in the north and southwest of the country. Flat land is better for farming. It is also easier to build roads and buildings on flat land. There are some low hills and valleys made by rivers there, too.

Canals link many rivers. Rivers and canals are used to move things from place to place, and for vacationers' boats.

This canal has been dug in the north of France, which is fairly flat.

WEATHER, PLANTS, AND ANIMALS

Summer in the south of France. People work, shop, and play games like boules (in the picture) in the cooler mornings or evenings.

THE WEATHER

Different parts of France have very different weather. The south has hot, dry summers and cool, wet winters. The north and west are cooler all year round.

It can be very cold in the east of France in winter. When the wind blows from the east, it brings cold air from the frozen parts of Russia. The mountains are coldest of all, with heavy snow in winter.

PLANTS AND ANIMALS

There are not many places in France where the land has not been cleared for homes or farming. Even much of the **scrubland** in the south has been cleared.

The mountains and the wet **marshlands** still have their natural plants, although some areas of marshland have been drained to use for farming.

There are not many wild animals left in France. There are some wolves and wild boar in the mountains.

The south of France has bad weather, too. It has rain storms in summer, and a strong wind called the Mistral can blow at up to 60 miles per hour.

The Carmargue marshland in the south of France. Many animals and birds live wild here. There are not many people in the Camargue.

TOWNS AND CITIES

OLD TOWNS

Many of the towns and cities in France are very old. Some of them were first built in the time of the **Roman Empire**.

PARIS

Paris is an old city. The old part is the center of the city, which has museums, art galleries, and old churches, as well as lots of stores and restaurants. This is the part of Paris that **tourists** visit.

A view of Paris and the Seine River. The center of Paris is a mixture of old and new buildings.

TOURISM AND INDUSTRY

French towns have grown for different reasons. Some towns are mainly factory towns. So, Lille is famous for fabric production. Other towns are busy ports, like Marseilles. Then there are the tourist towns, like the seaside town of Nice.

LOCAL FOCUS

France has many market towns that are important to the nearby villages. They are where the farmers go to sell their crops and animals, or to buy things they cannot get in their villages.

In France, three out of four people live in a town or city. Most of Europe is the same. In Italy and Portugal, more people live in rural areas.

Many tourists visit Cannes, in the south of France, especially when the annual film festival is on.

LIVING IN PARIS

THE DUPLEIX FAMILY

Tanguy and Claire Dupleix live in an apartment in the city of Paris. They have two boys, Leonard (age eleven) and Louis (age five) and two girls, Camille (age thirteen) and Clothilde (age seven).

The family's apartment is in an old building in the center of the city.

THE FAMILY'S DAY

Tanguy and Claire work all week. They work in the same office. Tanguy rides a motorcycle to work, because it is quick. The children go to school nearby.

Claire works part-time. She also has to shop and cook for the family.

It takes Camille and Leonard ten minutes to walk to school

Sometimes the family play Scrabble in the evening.

Camille and Leonard are practicing their music together.

MEALTIMES

The family has coffee, bread, and jam for breakfast. They have lunch at work or school. They eat their main meal in the evening. They like to eat meat cooked in sauces, and vegetables.

TIME OFF

The family lives on one of the big shopping streets in the city. There is a lot to see and do close to home. They can go to stores, restaurants, cafés, and parks.

The family likes to spend time together at home, too. They play board games, and the children play music. Tanguy also likes to jog to keep fit.

Tanguy rides his motorcycle to work.

13

FARMING IN FRANCE

French farmers grow all sorts of different crops, depending on the weather, the soil, and how high the land is.

GROWING WHEAT

Wheat grows best in the large, flat fields where it is easy to use plows and harvesters. Wheat needs soil that is not too dry. It needs rain to grow and sun to ripen.

KEEPING COWS

Cows are kept on dairy farms, for their milk. A lot of the milk is made into butter and cheese. French butter and cheese are famous all over the world.

Cows are raised in cool, wet areas where the grass grows well. Cows and sheep are also kept in places where it is too hilly to grow crops.

OTHER CROPS

The south of France is hot and dry. It is a good place to grow sweetcorn and sunflowers, which are used to make cooking oil.

MAKING WINE

Grapes are grown in vineyards all over France, but mostly in the warm, dry south. The grapes are used to make wine. French wine is famous, and each area of France makes its own kind of wine. Each wine looks, smells, and tastes different.

The grapes these people are picking will be made into wine.

People who know a lot about French wine can tell where it comes from by tasting and sniffing it. Sometimes they can even tell the name of the vineyard it came from!

LIVING IN THE COUNTRY

THE JUSSIAUX FAMILY

Dominique and Isabelle Jussiaux live in the country near Falaise. They have one girl, Camille, who is seven, and one boy, Thomas, who is four.

Isabelle and Dominique run a riding school, where children learn to ride horses. Isabelle is in charge of teaching riding. Dominique breeds and trains the horses so that they are safe to ride. The family has 40 horses in their stables. Isabelle and Camille both enter riding competitions in their spare time.

The family's house has a big yard and lots of land for the horses.

The family is eating pasta, rabbit stew, and cheese for their evening meal.

THE FAMILY'S DAY

While Isabelle and Dominique are working, Camille goes to elementary school and Thomas goes to nursery school. Isabelle drives them to school in Falaise, where she also shops for food.

MEALTIMES

The family eats bread with jam for breakfast. The children eat lunch at school, but the family eats together in the evening.

The horses are kept in stables, like these.

FRENCH STORES

SMALL STORES

France has lots of small stores that sell just one thing, like cheese or cakes. Very small stores in villages usually sell a bit of everything, but most villages have a separate bakery.

BIG STORES

There are also big supermarkets that sell everything. The biggest ones, called hypermarkets, are built on the edges of towns with lots of room for parking.

A hypermarket in France. They sell all sorts of things at lower prices than small stores.

Buying cheese from a market stall. Lots of the cheese is made by local farmers.

MARKETS

Some people still buy things from local markets, not supermarkets. Fruit and vegetables in the markets are often fresher because they have come straight from local farms.

OPENING HOURS

Small local stores open at about 9:00 A.M. and close for lunch. They then stay open into the late afternoon. They usually have a day in the week when they close. Hypermarkets open very early and close late in the evening, to get as many customers as possible.

Some French markets are in special market buildings, and others are open-air street markets with temporary stalls.

FRENCH FOOD

EATING OUT AND EATING IN

When French people go out to a big restaurant, they often eat large meals that take a long time to make. But there are also places that sell cheap, fast food.

When people eat at home, they often cook the main course, but get some of the food from special stores. They might have cold, cooked meats to start the meal, and tart or cake from a bakery to finish it.

Eating out in a restaurant. People often eat out with friends and will spend all evening eating a meal.

Most French butchers cut, roll, and put special stuffings in the meat for their customers.

BREAD

People eat bread with almost every meal. Bakers make lots of different breads.

SPECIAL FOODS

French food is eaten all over the world. Different parts of France are famous for different sorts of food. Places near the sea are famous for fish dishes. The area around the port of Marseilles is famous for fish soup. Normandy is famous for its apple tarts.

Bakers make croissants and brioches, too. These are sweet, rich breads, almost like cakes.

21

MADE IN FRANCE

France sells many **goods** to other countries, from food and drinks, to cars. **Exports** have made France rich.

FACTORIES

Some factories in France make things to sell, like cars. Others process food, like turning sunflowers into sunflower oil or putting milk into bottles. Others make steel. More than half the electricity that runs factories, homes, and offices is made in **nuclear power** stations.

This factory makes fuel for nuclear power stations.

CARS AND PLANES

French inventors worked on early types of cars and planes. French factories have been making cars and planes ever since. They try to use new designs and ideas, like using robots to build cars.

CLOTHES

Every year there are fashion shows in Paris. People come from all over the world to look at the clothes being shown.

Only Japan, the United States, and Germany make more cars each year than France.

23

GETTING AROUND

France has very good road, rail, sea, and **canal** routes for getting around. Most cities have airports, too.

RAILROADS

France has some of the world's fastest trains, even faster than Japanese "bullet" trains. French TGV trains can go as fast as 180 miles per hour.

Not all French trains are this fast. Local trains are slower.

TGV trains waiting in a Paris station. These trains run between Paris and Bordeaux.

Cities, like Paris, have a lot of traffic and air pollution.

ROADS AND TUNNELS

France has a very good road system. Special toll highways link the major cities. You have to pay to use them. There are also other long, straight highways that you do not need to pay to use. They join up main towns and cities.

Road and rail tunnels link France and other countries in Europe, including Italy, and England (by the Channel Tunnel).

RIVERS AND CANALS

Rivers, and the canals that join them, are used to move heavy **goods** around, especially in the north of France where there are more factories.

Paris has a subway system, the Metro. People use it to avoid road traffic, but it gets full, too.

SPORTS AND VACATIONS

SPORTS

Some French people like to watch and play tennis, soccer, golf, and rugby. Some important sporting events are held in France, like the Tour de France bicycle race, the Le Mans car race, and golf and tennis matches.

The Tour de France bicycle race is held every year. People come from all over the world to watch.

Many French people enjoy skiing. Many children learn to ski when they are very young.

Skiing brings many **tourists** to France. It is a popular sport for French people, too.

TIME OFF

People like to relax in cafés and bars, or go to the cinema or the theater. Boules is a popular game, played all over France. It is like a game of marbles using metal balls. Everyone tries to get closest to a target ball.

VACATIONS

Most French people take their vacation in August, when it is very hot. Many of them like to leave the towns and cities and go to the country or the coast for their vacation. People with young children might visit a theme park, like Disneyland Paris or Parc Asterix, both near Paris.

More than nine million people live in Paris. It is a big city. The Disneyland Paris theme park covers land one-fifth of the total size of Paris!

27

FESTIVALS AND ARTS

FESTIVALS

Some French festivals are religious, but many are not. Some festivals, like Easter, are celebrated all over France. Some are local farming or fishing celebrations.

On July 14, France celebrates Bastille Day, an important festival. It celebrates the French **Revolution** of 1789, which replaced kings with a **government** chosen by the people.

People celebrating Mardi Gras in Nice. The festival is just before Lent, when some Christians give things up until Easter.

This picture was painted by the famous French artist, Auguste Renoir, in 1876.

The first French artists lived about 30,000 years ago. They painted hunters and animals on the walls of caves. The paintings are still there.

ARTS

Many famous artists, sculptors, musicians, and writers have come from France. Art galleries all over the world have examples of French painting and sculpture. French artists are famous for trying out new ways of painting.

Famous French artists include Claude Monet, who liked to paint landscapes, and Paul Gauguin. Gauguin is famous for his brightly colored paintings of people in Polynesia.

FRANCE FACT FILE

People
People from France are called French.

Capital city
The capital city of France is Paris.

Largest cities
Paris is the largest city in France with more than nine million people. The second largest is Lyons. Marseilles is the third largest city.

Head of country
France is ruled by a president and a **government**.

Population
There are nearly 58 million people living in France.

Money
The money in France is called the franc.

Language
Nearly everyone speaks French. French uses the same letters as the English alphabet.

Religion
Three-quarters of French people are Catholic.

MORE BOOKS TO READ

Butler, Daphne. *France*. Austin, TX: Raintree Steck-Vaughn, 1992.

Wright, David and Wright, Jill. *France*. London: Evans; North Pomfret, Vermont: Trafalger, 1991.

GLOSSARY

canals These are manmade waterways.

exports These are goods sold to other countries.

goods These are things people have made.

gorge This is a steep, narrow valley made by a river or stream.

government These are the people who run the country. In France the government is elected by the people.

lava This is melted rock from a volcano.

marshland This is low land that is wet all the time and can flood in winter.

nuclear power This is energy that can be used as electricity that is created by nuclear reactions.

plateau This is a high, flat area of land.

revolution This is when the people in a country overthrow their rulers.

Roman Empire The Romans were people from Rome in Italy, who took over much of Europe and other parts of the world from 750 B.C. to 300 A.D.

scrubland This is a hot, dry place where only bushes and grass grow.

tourist This is someone who visits a place on a vacation.

volcano This is a mountain that sometimes throws out melted rock or ash.

INDEX